Guatemala

by Jessica Rudolph

Consultant: Marjorie Faulstich Orellana, PhD
Professor of Urban Schooling
University of California, Los Angeles

BEARPORT

Credits

TOC, © traveler1116/iStock; 4, © loca4motion/iStock; 5L, © age fotostock/Alamy; 5R, © fotoember/iStock; 7, © Urs FLUEELER/123RF; 8–9, © Stefan Ember/123RF; 9, © Stuart Gray/123RF; 10, © soft_light/Shutterstock; 11T, © Anan Kaewkhammul/Shutterstock; 11B, © Phoo Chan/Shutterstock; 12–13, © Simon Dannhauer/Shutterstock; 14–15, © cleanfotos/Shutterstock; 16, © Liba Taylor/Alamy; 17, © Pelonmaker/Shutterstock; 18, © Olivier Lantzendorffer/iStock; 19T, © Milosz_M/Shutterstock; 19B, © Colin13362/iStock; 20T, © Milosz_M/Shutterstock; 20B, © PKRF/Alamy; 21, © Katarzyna Citko/Shutterstock; 22, © Presse750/Dreamstime; 23L, © Maks Narodenko/Shutterstock; 23R, © Valentyn Volkov/Shutterstock; 24, © Roberto A Sanchez/iStock; 25L, © Roberto A Sanchez/iStock; 25R, © Fotos593/Shutterstock; 25B, © JuanSalvador/Shutterstock; 26–27, © loca4motion/Shutterstock; 28, © Phon Promwisate/Shutterstock; 29, © Photo Works/Shutterstock; 30 (T to B), © fourleaflover/Shutterstock, © Amelia Johnson/Thinkstock, © Sementer/Shutterstock, and © John Vizcaino/Reuters/Corbis; 31 (T to B), © Olivier Lantzendorffer/iStock, © Milosz_M/Shutterstock, © Valentyn Volkov/Shutterstock, and © soft_light/Shutterstock; 32, © Gwoeii/Shutterstock.

Publisher: Kenn Goin
Editor: J. Clark
Creative Director: Spencer Brinker
Design: Debrah Kaiser
Photo Researcher: Olympia Shannon

Library of Congress Cataloging-in-Publication Data

Rudolph, Jessica.
  Guatemala / by Jessica Rudolph.
    pages cm. — (Countries we come from)
  Includes bibliographical references and index.
  Audience: Ages 4–8.
  ISBN 978-1-62724-856-3 (library binding) — ISBN 1-62724-856-0 (library binding)
  1. Guatemala—Juvenile literature. I. Title.
  F1463.2.R83 2016
  972.81—dc23
                                2015004753

For more information, write to Bearport Publishing Company, Inc., 45 West 21st Street, Suite 3B, New York, New York 10010. Printed in the United States of America.

10 9 8 7 6 5 4 3 2 1

Contents

This Is Guatemala

Colorful

Busy

WARM

Guatemala is a country in Central America.

More people live there than in any other country in Central America.

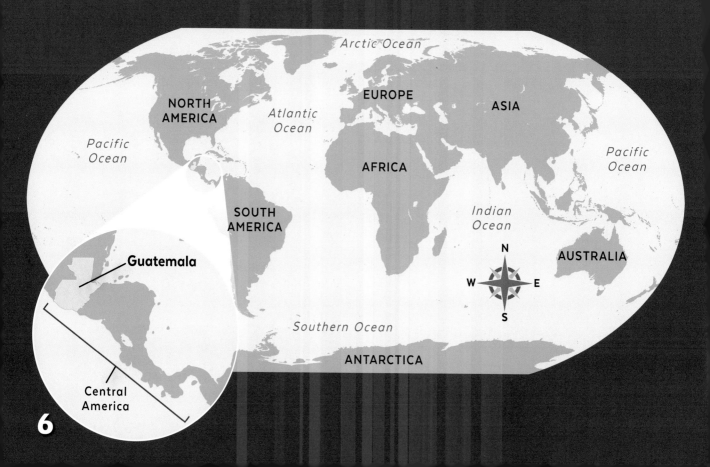

More than 15 million people live in Guatemala.

Guatemala has many beautiful mountains.

It also has lots of volcanoes.

A volcano named Fuego sends out some smoke every day.

There are **rain forests** in Guatemala.

They get almost 200 inches (5 m) of rain a year.

Jaguars and many other animals live in the rain forests.

Quetzals (KWET–zulhz) also live in the rain forests. These birds have tail feathers up to 3 feet (0.9 m) long!

Tikal stands in a rain forest.

A group of people called the Maya built this city about 2,000 years ago.

Nobody lives in Tikal anymore.

However, today Maya people live all over Guatemala.

The Maya built giant stone buildings at Tikal. Visitors come to see the buildings.

The Spanish came to Guatemala in the 1500s.

They ruled for 300 years.

Today, most Guatemalans are part Spanish and part Maya.

The Spanish built many churches. Some of the churches are still used today.

Mayan languages and Spanish are spoken in Guatemala.

In Spanish, the word for *hello* is:

Hola (OH-lah)

The word for *good-bye* is:

Adiós (ah-dee-YOHS)

road signs in Spanish

More than 20 Mayan languages are spoken in Guatemala.

About half of Guatemalans live in cities.

Guatemala City is the largest.

It's also the country's **capital**.

Outdoor markets are popular in towns and cities. People can buy fresh food at markets. They can also buy handmade **crafts** such as blankets and wooden masks.

The weather in Guatemala is warm all year.

Many kinds of **crops** grow in the warm weather.

Farmers grow corn, beans, and other foods.

Farmers also raise pigs and cows.

About half of Guatemalans work on farms.

a worker on a coffee farm

Some Guatemalan crops are sold in other countries.

Coffee and bananas from Guatemala are sold in the United States.

Tortillas are a popular food.

They are thin, round, and made from corn.

Guatemalans eat tortillas with most meals.

Tortillas can be folded around meat or eaten plain.

Many people also like to eat a sweet bread called pan dulce.

Guatemalans celebrate lots of holidays.

People go to cemeteries on All Saints' Day.

They honor those who have died.

They put flowers on graves.

Some people celebrate this day by flying huge kites.

kites

flowers on a grave

27

What do people do for fun?

Many play sports!

Soccer is very popular.

In Guatemala, soccer is called fútbol (FOOT-bohl).

Fast Facts

Capital city:
Guatemala City

Population of Guatemala:
15.6 million

Main language: Spanish

Money: Quetzal

Major religions:
Christian and Maya religions

Neighboring countries: Mexico, Belize,
Honduras, and El Salvador

Cool Fact: Rigoberta Menchú Tum is a famous Maya leader from Guatemala. She won an award called the Nobel Peace Prize for her work to help the Maya people.

capital (KAP-uh-tuhl) a city where a country's government is based

crafts (KRAFTS) art or other objects that take skill to make

crops (KROPS) plants that are grown in large amounts, usually for food

rain forests (RAYN FOR-ists) warm places where many trees grow and lots of rain falls

Index

Read More

Aboff, Marcie. *Guatemala ABCs: A Book About the People and Places of Guatemala (Country ABCs).* Minneapolis, MN: Picture Window Books (2006).

Schuetz, Kari. *Guatemala (Blastoff! Readers: Exploring Countries).* Minneapolis, MN: Bellwether Media (2012).

Learn More Online

To learn more about Guatemala, visit
www.bearportpublishing.com/CountriesWeComeFrom

About the Author

Jessica Rudolph lives in Connecticut. She has edited and written many books about history, science, and nature for children.